# THE EEYOU
## PEOPLE OF EASTERN JAMES BAY

# THE EEYOU

## PEOPLE OF EASTERN JAMES BAY

by

ALEXANDRA SIY

DILLON PRESS
New York

Maxwell Macmillan Canada
Toronto

Maxwell Macmillan International
New York  Oxford  Singapore  Sydney

## PHOTO CREDITS

Cover photos courtesy of Patti D'Angelo
Gretchen McHugh: Title page, 40, 52, 59, 69; Colin Scott: 12, 33, 35, 37, 39, 44, 48, 49, 50, 51, 57; Luc Beaulé: 16-17, 46, 47; Frederic Remington/National Archives of Canada: 19; Hudson's Bay Company Archives: 22; Patti D'Angelo: 25, 26, 61, 63; Lieutenant Hood R. N./National Archives of Canada: 29.

The author wishes to thank the James Bay Cree Cultural Education Centre for its gracious permission to publish the following material from copyrighted works: "Mitchsiiaau and the Indian" from *Aatiyuuhkaan: Legends of the Eastern James Bay Cree*, copyright 1989; the tale about fishnets from *Cree Trappers Speak*, copyright 1989; and the beluga whale story from *Cree Trappers Speak*, copyright 1989.

Book design by Carol Matsuyama

## LIBRARY OF CONGRESS CATALOGING-IN-PUBLICATION DATA

Siy, Alexandra.
    The Eeyou : people of eastern James Bay / by Alexandra Siy. – 1st ed.
      p.  cm. – (Global villages)
    Includes bibliographical references.
    Summary: Describes the history, language, and culture of the Eeyou, or Cree Indians of Eastern James Bay in northern Quebec, and discusses how their way of life is threatened by hydroelectric projects.
    ISBN 0-87518-549-5
    1. Cree Indians–Social life and customs–Juvenile literature. 2. James Bay (Ont. and Quebec)–Social life and customs–Juvenile I. Title. II. Series.
    E99.C88S59    1993
    971.4'115–dc20                       92-34887

Dillon Press
Macmillan Publishing Company
866 Third Avenue
New York, NY 10022

Maxwell Macmillan Canada, Inc.
1200 Eglinton Avenue East
Suite 200
Don Mills, Ontario M3C 3N1

Macmillan Publishing Company is part of the Maxwell Communication Group of Companies.

First edition

Printed in the United States of America
10  9  8  7  6  5  4  3  2  1

## ACKNOWLEDGMENTS

Many people shared their knowledge and time with me, and I sincerely thank all of them for their contributions. I extend special thanks to Janie Pachano, director of the James Bay Cree Cultural Education Centre, for providing me with research materials, for sharing important insights, and for reading drafts of the manuscript. Special thanks also to Luci Salt and Danielle Mukash, who both provided important information (including writings by Cree students) and took time to read drafts and make suggestions.

I would like to extend my gratitude also to Dr. Richard Preston, professor of anthropology at McMaster University in Hamilton, Ontario, for his assistance.

The following people and their organizations made important contributions to this project: Michel Dorais (Canadian Federal Environmental Assessment Review Office), Leon-Marie Hachez (Hydro-Quebec), Valerie Langer (Cultural Survival Canada), Robbie Matthew (Cree Trappers Association), Bill Namagoose (executive director of the Cree Regional Authority), Shiela Mendonca (National Archives of Canada), Nancy Pfirman (James Bay Action Network), Carol Piciullo (Northeast Alliance to Protect James Bay), Marie Reidke (Hudson's Bay Company Archives), and Deborah Williams (Hulbert Outdoor Center).

Thanks also to the following individuals: Luc Beaulé, Arlene Clements, Margaret Cromarty, Patti D'Angelo, Ted Levin, Gretchen McHugh, and Boyce Richardson.

I also wish to thank my editor, Joyce Stanton, for her good judgment and patience. And, finally, thanks to Eric Siy, my husband, who contributed his professional comments and insight, and provided me with much patience and love during the project.

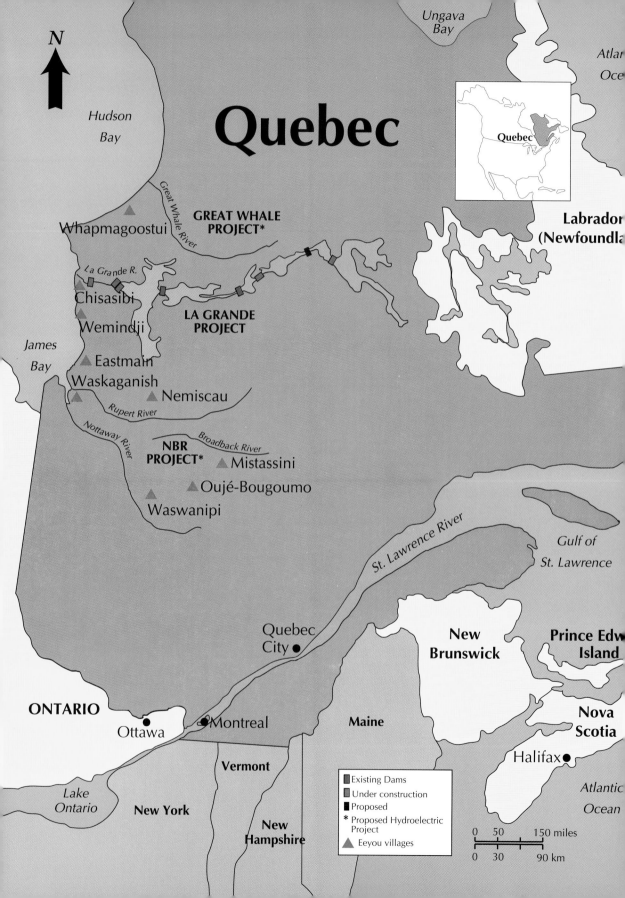

# CONTENTS

# INTRODUCTION

As the 1990s draw to a close, we look forward to not only a new century but a new millennium. What will the next thousand years bring for the planet earth and its people? And what aspects of our ancient past will we retain on our journey into a new time, a new world?

Today the world is already a vastly different place from what our great-grandparents would have imagined. People from distant parts of the planet can communicate within seconds. In less than 24 hours you can fly around the world. Thanks to these and other remarkable advances in technology, the world has become a "global village."

In a sense, the peoples of the earth are no longer strangers, but neighbors. As we meet our "neighbors," we learn that now, more than ever before, our lives are intertwined. Indeed, our survival may depend on one another.

Far to the north, in the subarctic regions of eastern Canada, the Eeyou, or Cree Indians, have lived for 6,000 years. Europeans first came to their land in the 17th century, establishing a thriving fur trade and bringing many changes to the people's way of life. Until now, the Eeyou have managed to adapt to many of the changes, but today the development of hydroelectric projects threatens their existence. As rivers are dammed and their courses diverted, Cree lands are being lost beneath floodwaters, fish are being contaminated, and wildlife necessary to the people's survival is being destroyed. The industrialized world's demand for electricity has produced, for the Cree, an ecosystem out of balance.

It need not happen. Plans for the projects can be changed, and people in both societies–modern and traditional–can find that being part of a global village can enrich their lives. As we learn about other cultures, we may discover much about our own. And as we get to know our neighbors, we may find new ways to understand and respect all people.

# FAST FACTS

### CULTURE
The Eeyou live by hunting both large and small game, birds, and sea mammals; fishing in both fresh and salt waters; and trapping fur mammals.

### HUMAN HISTORY
The first Eeyou, or Cree Indians, settled in the subarctic region near James Bay perhaps as early as 6,000 years ago, when the great Ice Age glacier melted off the land. The first known European contact with the Eeyou occurred in 1611. The Eeyou traded with the Hudson's Bay Company for more than 300 years. Today the Eeyou live in and around nine villages on James and Hudson bays and number more than 10,000 people.

### NATURAL HISTORY
The glacier melted about 6,000 years ago in the James Bay–Hudson Bay lowlands region, creating an environment of lakes, bogs, rivers, tundra, and evergreen forests.

### GEOGRAPHY
The subarctic is the land surrounding the Arctic Circle. In North America the subarctic stretches from Labrador in the east to Alaska in the west.

### CLIMATE
Very cold in winter, averaging −10°F in January; warm but short summers, averaging 65°F in July; dry, averaging 23 inches total snow- and rainfall.

### GLOBAL IMPORTANCE
The region is the home of the Eeyou, the largest group of indigenous hunters left in North America. Part of the Hudson Bay bioregion, the area provides habitat for great herds of caribou and the largest beluga whale

population in the world. It includes breeding and feeding grounds for hundreds of species of migratory birds. Most of the earth's rare freshwater seals live in the region's lakes. It is Canada's largest wetland, with some of the greatest expanses of uncut forests in the world.

## CURRENT STATUS

The way of life of the Eeyou is threatened by hydroelectric develop-ment in the area. James Bay I, which dammed the La Grande River, is a hydroelectric complex that covers an area the size of the six New England states. The proposed James Bay II would dam the Great Whale River and the Nottaway, Broadback, and Rupert rivers. A total of 20 power stations would be built and almost 7,000 square miles of land flooded, changing an ecosystem the size of France.

*The Eeyou have made their home deep in the frigid forests of northeastern Canada for 6,000 years.*

# FIRST PEOPLE

 In a forest clearing the sound of a drum rises from a glowing teepee. A chanting voice is heard above the drumbeat, singing in rhythms of past, present, and future. The words are not fully understood, but meanings are felt deep to the core of all who listen. The songs are ancient, connecting the voices of the present to voices belonging to people who lived in these forests thousands of years ago.

All over the world there are **tribes** of people whose ancestors were the first to live in a certain place. Known today as **indigenous** peoples, they are the descendants of the very first people who lived on tribal lands.

The land first seen, first touched, first inhabited by ancient people is the same land that provides their descendants with the things needed for life. Indigenous people can see the faces of these ancient ones in their own grandparents, parents, and children. **Traditions, rituals,** songs, stories, and especially the land itself are the links the first people of today have to the first people of long ago.

Today, the voices of indigenous peoples are being heard

around the world. They tell us things about our history and our earth we may have known but not really understood.

## THE EEYOU

Canada's **subarctic** north is home to a group of first people. They call themselves Eeyou (EE-you), the word in their language that simply means "people." To outsiders they are known as the Cree Indians, and they have lived deep in the forests and along the shores of eastern James Bay for about 6,000 years.

## AFTER THE GLACIER

The first Eeyou settled in the eastern James Bay region after the last glacier melted northward. There they found a cold land of evergreen forests, mountains, **bogs**, and **tundra**. They lived by hunting large animals, such as bear, caribou, and moose. Smaller animals, fish, and plants were also part of their diet.

The Eeyou lived in shelters made of bark and animal skins, and they traveled in search of food. Their survival depended on their movement over large areas of land, and on cooperation with one another.

For thousands of years there were many hundreds of small groups, or bands, of Eeyou. These people were not ruled by a chief or other leaders. Instead an expert hunter, with the help of **elders**, gave advice to the band. Known as the *auchimau,* this hunter decided who would hunt in different areas of the forest.

The Eeyou were **hunter-gatherers**, surviving on the food they hunted and gathered from the land. They believed that the people belonged to the land. Land could not be owned by people, but the people had the responsibility to care for the land and the animals. This responsibility was passed from hunter to hunter over many generations.

In the Cree language the word *nitibaaihtaan* means to take care of the land and animals as a steward or custodian. Even today the Eeyou do not believe they own the land on which they live. Instead they believe they are the people who know how to best care for the land.

## ARRIVAL OF THE EUROPEANS

During ancient times the Eeyou needed a few important tools, weapons, and warm clothing to survive in the subarctic. Everything they used was made from readily available materials. Parts of animals and trees were used to make tents, spears, scrapers, bows and arrows, cooking equipment, clothing, boats, sleds, snowshoes, and musical instruments. They survived by using only the animals and plants that lived around them.

Then, nearly 400 years ago, the Eeyou were introduced to tools that changed their **Stone Age** culture forever. In 1611 the English explorer Henry Hudson arrived on the shore of James Bay. He was nearly frozen to death, but was able to trade his knife, a mirror, and some buttons for two beaver pelts in which he

*The Eeyou have survived by hunting large animals like caribou.*

wrapped himself. The person he traded with was a Cree Indian.

By the late 1600s the Cree were well-established trading partners with the French and English. The Indians exchanged beaver pelts for knives, axes, metal scrapers and fishhooks, brass kettles, rifles, blankets, and eventually steel animal traps. The Europeans sailed home with the furs, where they were made into hats and other garments.

## THE HUDSON'S BAY COMPANY

Most of the Indians did not trade directly with the Europeans. These Eeyou remained isolated in the **bush**, where they hunted, trapped, and fished. Occasionally, they obtained steel tools by trading with Eeyou known as the "home guard" or "coasters," who lived near the trading posts along the coasts. The home guard sometimes acted as middlemen–obtaining furs from other Indians and, in return, supplying them with European tools and other items. The home guard also hunted for the fur traders and were therefore the first Eeyou to use guns.

In 1670 the Hudson's Bay Company, or HBC, was established under a royal charter from the British government. The HBC became a rich and powerful company, profiting from the fine furs brought to the trading posts by the Indians. For more than 300 years, the Hudson's Bay Company operated small trading posts throughout Canada. These posts were usually unheated buildings located on rivers, such as Rupert House on the Rupert

*Fur traders on their way to an Indian camp. The Eeyou exchanged beaver pelts for steel implements, rifles, blankets, and other European products.*

River. Furs were brought to the posts by canoe and carried back to England in large trading ships.

## CHANGING TIMES

For the next 200 years the Eeyou experienced gradual changes that affected their way of life, or **culture**. More and more Eeyou gave up traditional tools made of bone, wood, and stone for steel axes, knives, traps, and shotguns. Wool blankets and cloth garments sometimes replaced furs and animal skins. And new foods such as flour and sugar were used occasionally in cooking. These changes were usually regarded by the Eeyou as laborsaving.

Some historians believe the fur trade made the Eeyou dependent on the Europeans. But others argue that the Indians did not really lose their independence because they never lost the **traditional** knowledge and skills they needed to survive.

Along with the helpful new tools from Europe came changes that were harmful to the Eeyou. The fur traders introduced the Indians to rum, brandy, and other alcoholic drinks. Native people had no experience with alcohol. As a result, even small amounts could cause intoxication.

Despite many changes, the Eeyou were able to maintain their traditional way of life. Almost all the people lived in the bush, and most used only a few new tools to help them with their daily work. But most important, the traditional beliefs that defined the Eeyou culture remained unchanged. New tools may have altered the way some things were done, but the Eeyou did not change their ancient beliefs about their place in the natural world.

These beliefs were very different from those held by the Europeans. While the Eeyou thought people were part of nature and should live in balance and harmony with all living things, the Europeans thought humans should conquer and dominate nature. And while the Eeyou cherished the belief of *nitibaaihtaan* and lived in a way that cared for the land and its creatures, the Europeans claimed ownership of the land and wanted to make a profit from its animals and other resources.

## HARD TIMES

By the late 1800s **missionaries** had established churches and schools in the villages that had slowly developed around the trading posts. Their purpose, or mission, was to convert the Indians into followers of Christ.

For the first time in their history, most of the Eeyou remained in villages during the summer, where they worked as summer laborers and **voyageurs**. Many Eeyou also attended church and school. During this period, a large number were converted to Christianity. Although these Eeyou accepted the Christian faith, they did not abandon their traditional spiritual beliefs. Instead they found that the basic teachings of Christianity were similar to their own: the belief in a single creator, the existence of an afterlife, and the responsibility of people to care for one another and the earth.

But the short time spent in summer villages had a destructive effect on the Eeyou. Prolonged contact with the missionaries and fur traders caused many people to become ill and die from European diseases, such as flu and measles. Relatively harmless to Europeans, these diseases were deadly to the Eeyou, who had no natural resistance against them.

Adding to the stress of foreign disease was the sudden decline in the beaver and caribou populations. By 1920 beavers were nearly extinct in the region, and many Eeyou starved.

Historians aren't exactly sure why these important animals became scarce so suddenly. The Eeyou know that most subarctic animals experience population cycles. During some years certain animals are scarce and at other times are abundant. Probably a

*Rupert House in the 1890s. For more than 300 years, the Hudson's Bay Company operated small trading posts like this one throughout Canada.*

combination of natural population cycles and excessive hunting and trapping by non-native people contributed to the disaster.

Between 1920 and 1940 hundreds of Eeyou died, mainly from tuberculosis, flu, measles, whooping cough, and bronchitis. The Hudson's Bay Company provided little relief, and the Canadian government believed it was a waste of money to provide health care for people who lived in the bush.

Troubled by the suffering of the Eeyou, the missionaries asked the government to take more responsibility for health care. Some Hudson's Bay employees also tried to help the Eeyou as much as they could. For example, Maud Watt, the wife of the Rupert House HBC manager, cared for many sick Eeyou at the trading post.

Maud Watt also convinced the government to set aside a large area of Cree territory where only Eeyou could trap and hunt. In 1932 a beaver preserve was established that was off-limits to non-native hunters. By 1940 beavers were plentiful again.

During the 1940s immunizations and medicines were developed to prevent or fight the epidemics. By the early 1950s a hospital and a nursing station were built to serve the Eeyou. Although the Eeyou welcomed lifesaving inoculations and medicines, many people were not reached by the limited health program.

## FORGOTTEN PEOPLE

Between 1950 and 1970 the Eeyou acquired more modern technology, such as boat motors and snowmobiles. Yet they still lacked the basic health-care and educational services that all other Canadian citizens took for granted. The health-care services that were available were not sufficient, and they were run by outsiders who had no understanding of the people's culture or language.

The Eeyou also had no educational choices for their children. They could attend only distant boarding schools where the children were forbidden to speak their native language and were sometimes beaten. The goal of the schools was to strip the Eeyou of their culture and force them to live in the ways of the dominant Canadian culture. When these children returned to their families, they lacked the traditional skills needed for living in the bush. Many felt they had lost their identities.

Until the late 1960s the Eeyou and the land on which they lived were pretty much forgotten by the government. Few people knew or cared about the Eeyou and the sometimes desperate conditions they faced. Then, in 1971, the government of Quebec announced "the project of the century." Suddenly the land of the Eeyou was to be part of the biggest engineering feat on earth.

The plan, now known as James Bay I, was to dam the huge La Grande River and build several hydroelectric generating stations along its rapids. The electricity generated from the stations would be transmitted hundreds of miles south to Montreal and cities in the United States. The government didn't even notify the Eeyou of its plans. Instead the Eeyou learned of the project from a radio report.

## FIGHTING BACK

Outraged at the prospect that their ancient hunting and burial grounds would be flooded and destroyed forever, the Eeyou decided to fight back. Fifty Eeyou and Inuit (Eskimo) hunters protested in the Quebec courts against the project. The Inuit live in northernmost Quebec, along Hudson and Ungava bays.

The hunters convinced the judge that their way of life would be threatened if the river were dammed. But a week after their

*The beginning of James Bay I, the massive hydroelectric project along the La Grande River. The system of dams threatens to destroy the land and culture of the Eeyou.*

victory, the Eeyou learned that a higher court had decided that the project would be built anyway.

The Eeyou did not stop fighting for their lands and their traditional way of life. They organized and chose leaders for the first time in their history. And they negotiated with the Canadian government about the future of their remaining lands.

In 1975 the Eeyou signed the James Bay and Northern Quebec Agreement. This was a historic treaty because it recognized that the Eeyou had the same rights, such as quality health care and education, as other Canadians. The treaty also stated that the Eeyou would decide how their lands would be used in

*For the first time in their history, the Eeyou organized and chose leaders to fight for their lands.*

the future. But despite this treaty, the Eeyou are threatened by a second major hydroelectric project.

## THE EEYOU TODAY . . . AND TOMORROW

Today there are nine Cree villages scattered over northern Quebec. Each village has a chief. The villages are united by a grand chief and the Grand Council of the Crees of Quebec. The Cree Regional Authority runs programs such as health care and education.

Most families now live year-round in villages, where there are schools and stores. During the winter children go to Cree schools where they speak their native language and learn traditional skills. Many families travel into the bush for several weeks during the winter to trap and hunt. And some Eeyou have chosen to live all winter in the bush and spend only the summers in the villages.

In spite of many changes, the Eeyou still live by most of the same traditions as their ancestors. Values, spiritual beliefs, traditional foods, and ceremonies have been nurtured and kept by the elders and passed on to the new generation.

Today the youngest Eeyou are faced with decisions and challenges that will determine the future of their ancient culture. Their world is two worlds–the traditional hunting culture of their ancestors and the modern world of industrialized Canada.

## THE GLOBAL VILLAGE

The Eeyou continue their struggle to prevent the construction of new dams, power stations, and roads on their lands. But that struggle is not theirs alone. It affects all of us because we are part of one world. Technology has made rapid communication across our planet easy, bringing the world closer together. What happens in one part of the globe affects other areas.

Today our world is a **global village**–a place where all people seek respect and freedom, share common needs, and face worldwide problems, such as threats to the environment. Perhaps as modern nations strive to solve complicated problems, it would help to understand how some native cultures live in harmony with their surroundings.

# CHAPTER TWO

# A RHYTHM OF LIFE

ᒥᒥ ᒎ°   *Ki tepaciman weskit tapwe*—"Here is a story from long, long ago."

## "MITCHSIIAAU AND THE INDIAN"

One night a man was sleeping in his tent. A sound woke him up. He looked out of his tent and saw a giant bird named Mitchsiiaau.

"It's me, Grandson," said the bird.

"What is the matter, Grandfather?" asked the man anxiously. The man thought the bird might hurt him.

"I can't hurt anyone. I grabbed a rock last night thinking it was an animal, and now my claws are broken."

The man gave Mitchsiiaau four beavers to eat.

"Thank you, Grandson," said Mitchsiiaau.

"Let me look at your claws, Grandfather," said the man. "I will try to fix them."

The man cut off the broken claws and sharpened the tips. "I think my claws are almost as they were before," Mitchsiiaau said. "Thank you, Grandson." And the bird left to try out his claws.

That night the man heard a noise outside the tent. He looked out and saw a big caribou dead at his feet.

*Stories told 'round the fire on long, cold winter nights have kept the ancient culture of the Eeyou alive.*

"It's for you, Grandson," Mitchsiiaau told the man. "You helped me tremendously. My claws work well and I can hunt again. For your help I also give you this warning: Your grandmother wants to catch you for her meal. You must never go out at night and never cross a lake–follow the shore instead. Your grandmother wants you very badly and she will be watching for a chance to catch you out in the open."

Mitchsiiaau flew away, and the man obeyed his warning. But one day the man was returning from trapping beaver, carrying a beaver on his back. He wanted to get home quickly and decided to run across the frozen lake.

He ran as fast as he could, but he was still far from his camp when he heard Mitchsiiaau's wife overhead. The bird lunged at the man and her claws sank into the beaver on his back. The bird carried the man into the sky and over his camp. Below, the people heard the man singing about his fate.

"My grandmother has caught me," he sang.

The bird flew to a high cliff and tried to smash the man against the rocks. But the man held his ice pick so that the handle was toward the cliff and the blade against the bird. The pick acted as a wedge between the cliff and the bird, saving the man.

Then the bird brought the man to her nest.

"I warned you that your grandmother would bring you here if she could," said Mitchsiiaau.

"Help me," said the man.

"I cannot," said Mitchsiiaau. "Your grandmother is much quicker than I. Test us and see."

The man threw a stick from the cliff and both birds flew to fetch it. The grandmother returned first and she had the stick in her claws.

The man knew his grandmother would eat him if he didn't do something quickly.

"I am going to make your home warm so that you won't get cold," the man told the birds. All around the nest he put wood and covered the top, too. He told the birds to go inside with their children to test if it was warm.

"Yes, it's warm," they said. They were tired from playing the man's game and they were happy with their home. So the grandmother decided to wait until morning to eat the man. When the birds were asleep, the man set fire to the nest. All the birds died.

The man took Mitchsiiaau's body and gutted it. He rolled the body to the cliff's edge and got inside. "Grandfather, you will try to save me now," he said. He rolled down the cliff and finally landed on the ground.

"My grandfather did save me," said the man. "What am I going to do with him?"

He thought a minute and then decided to cut up his grandfather's body into different-sized pieces. He threw the pieces into the air. These pieces became the clawed birds of all kinds and sizes. The bigger parts became clawed birds that hunt: owls, hawks, eagles, falcons. Some of these birds are eaten by us, and others, like the very large ones, are not.

## TURNING SEASONS

The Eeyou hunt the snowy owl only in October. Also known as "northern chicken," this bird of prey is considered a delicacy. The Eeyou understand the life cycles of all the birds and animals they hunt and trap. There is a season for everything. And as seasons unfold into years, the cycle of life repeats itself over and over.

Many people think of seasons as changes in the weather. But to the Eeyou, weather is only a part of the way one season changes to the next. The cold subarctic climate creates seasons that are much different from those in the rest of North America.

# THE EEYOU

Spring and summer are warm but very short, lasting from June to August. Snow can fall in September, and the lakes are frozen from November until May. The average temperature in January is −10°F.

Seasons for the Eeyou are characterized not only by climate changes, but also by the life cycles of certain animals and birds. In response to these cycles, the Eeyou have seasons for trapping, hunting, and fishing. However, these seasons do overlap–for example, some hunting is done during the trapping season, and fishing can be done all year long. Seasons for different activities also vary from band to band depending on where each group lives. For example, the activities of Eeyou living near the coast are different from those of Eeyou living inland.

Although many Eeyou live in villages during the winter, they still depend on the animals trapped and hunted in the bush. Often the men will go into the bush and bring **game** back to the villages to be shared among the people. Some families spend part of the winter in the bush, while others still live there all winter. Whatever living arrangement is chosen, the Eeyou depend on the traditional seasonal cycles for their survival.

## THE TRAPPING SEASON

The trapping season begins in September and ends in March. The most important fur animal is the beaver. Others include the lynx, otter, muskrat, mink, weasel, marten, red fox, arctic fox, wolf, and red squirrel.

*A trapper removes excess water from a dead beaver by dragging its body back and forth over the snow.*

The prime time for trapping beaver begins in November and continues through March. Beavers live in streams and lakes inside lodges made of sticks. A trapper taps the ice to find tunnels leading to a beaver lodge. Then he sets a trap under the ice at the entrance to the lodge. Before traps were available, beavers were killed with arrows, captured with baglike nets, or pulled by hand from lodges.

A trapper knows about how many beavers live in a lodge just by looking at it. He can also guess the ages of the beavers living there. Using this knowledge, he carefully plans how many and what types of beaver he will take from a lodge each year. Leaving animals alive in the lodge will help ensure a healthy beaver population year after year.

In November most trappers stay in their winter base camp and harvest the beavers and other fur animals that live nearby. For the rest of the winter they travel away from the camp and stay in temporary shelters. They return to the base camp every few weeks, where they leave the animals they've caught.

## THE WINTER CAMP

At the winter camp the Eeyou live in *muhtukan*, or rectangular-shaped houses made of logs and sod. Cracks between the logs are stuffed with moss to keep out the bitter winds. The floors are made of spruce branches laid on the sandy ground. Sweet smelling and soft, spruce branches make the lodge a warm and

*A muhtukan in a winter camp. The house, made of logs and sod, is roomy enough to shelter four families.*

inviting home for the winter.

*Muhtukan* are big enough for four families. Each family has its own corner of the lodge but shares the cooking fire and responsibilities for keeping the camp running smoothly.

Sometimes teepees are built instead of lodges–usually in warmer weather. A frame of poles is set up and covered with canvas. A fire or stove is placed in the center of a teepee and smoke escapes out the hole in the top. Traditionally, teepees were covered with caribou skins.

When the men go into the bush for days and weeks at a time, they build temporary shelters called *michwaup*. Shaped like a teepee, a *michwaup* is made out of logs and spruce boughs.

## THE HUNTING SEASON

April to October are the months during which most hunting takes place. Spring is the time when the first **migratory** birds, such as geese and ducks, return from warm southern climates. Hunters start taking these birds in April. May is known as loon month because red-throated loons, as well as many kinds of ducks, are plentiful. Some people collect duck eggs, too. The last months for duck and goose hunting are September and October–before the birds fly south again for the winter.

Eeyou who live near the coast hunt beluga whales in James Bay during June and July. In October seals are hunted from canoes until the water freezes in November.

Large game, such as bear and caribou, which provide a lot of food, are very important to the Eeyou. Bears are also respected as powerful animals. They are hunted in late August and early fall. During this time black bears are fat from eating berries all summer long. In November hunters look for **hibernating** black bears in dens.

Caribou hunting begins in October. One caribou provides meat for many families, and the skins are important for making clothing, tents, and bedding. Caribou are hunted all winter. If a hunter sees caribou tracks while out trapping, he will make a special effort to track the animals. Fresh caribou meat brought back to the winter camp is cause for celebration.

Other animals are hunted throughout the winter and into

*Spruce boughs, sweet smelling and soft, carpet the sandy floor of the muhtukan.*

the spring months. Porcupines, rabbits, spruce grouse, and ptarmigan, a bird that changes its feathers from brown in summer to white in winter, are hunted by the men while out trapping. Women and children also hunt these smaller animals near the base camp. By April hunters no longer take ptarmigan and spruce grouse–this is the time when the female birds prepare to lay and hatch their eggs.

## THE FISHING SEASON

The Eeyou have always depended on fish as an important part of their diet. Traditionally, ice fishing in winter provided the Eeyou

*In the spring, hunters capture geese and other migratory birds.*

with food when animals were scarce. Fish caught in winter sometimes saved families from starvation.

In the past, when all Eeyou spent the winter in the bush, summer was a time for groups of families to gather together. Every summer families met at special fishing places along the coasts, rivers, or lakes. This was an important time for relaxation after long months of trapping and hunting.

Today most Eeyou still gather at ancient fishing places during the summer for fishing, feasts, and ceremonies. And all the people–men, women, and children–enjoy fishing. Nets are used to catch more than a dozen kinds of fish, such as whitefish, trout, arctic char, pike, sturgeon, and longnose sucker.

## ANCIENT KNOWLEDGE

The Eeyou have acquired detailed knowledge over many centuries about the animals on which they depend for survival. Traditionally, this knowledge was not recorded in books because the Eeyou did not have a written language until the 1800s. Instead oral history–stories and legends handed down from generation to generation–has preserved this important information.

The skills needed for living in the bush require hard work and practice to master. In the past children were not taught how to do things; they learned by watching and through experience. Today children are taught traditional skills in school and also learn by watching the elders, living in the bush, and listening to stories.

Stories told during long cold winter nights in the bush were valuable for educating the children and were also good entertainment. Both in the past and today, stories are not taken lightly and are even considered sacred. They are from another world–another time. During storytelling the children listen quietly.

By listening to stories, the new generation of Eeyou are connected with the past. They can feel and visualize the world of long ago. And they can learn about the origins of things. Stories connect the inventions and discoveries of the past with the activities that people still do in their daily lives.

An old man tells a short story. The child who listens will tell the same story again, many years later:

*A hunter skins a caribou, one of the big game animals the Eeyou depend on for food.*

An old man was wandering in the bush. In the back of his mind, he was trying to figure out how to make a fishnet. He saw a spider. He stopped and watched how the spider was constructing his web. When he returned to his camp, he said to himself, Now I know how a spider constructs his web. I wonder if it would work if I constructed my fishnet in the same fashion? So he got to work, and sure enough, his net worked. Later he elaborated on his fishnet, added floats and sinkers, tried different mesh sizes. But that is how it all started—he just needed the inspiration to put it all together. And he got that from the spider.

# CHAPTER THREE

# THE ANCIENT DRUMBEAT

 Land and language. Both are essential for the survival of the Eeyou. The land is everything physical, everything material. It is food, water, shelter, clothing, and fire. And language is everything else. Language preserves the knowledge, traditions, rituals, and roles of the people. When a people lose their language, they lose their culture.

One way language is preserved over long periods of time is through ancient songs. For thousands of years, drums and songs stirred the souls of the Eeyou. But the drums were silenced by outsiders who believed they were evil.

In the 1800s missionaries burned the drums belonging to the Eeyou. The missionaries had little understanding of the native culture and thought that by destroying the drums they could change the people's spiritual beliefs.

## NEW DRUMS, ANCIENT SONGS

Today the Eeyou are making new drums. And the elders are singing the ancient songs to the sounds of these new drums for all to hear and learn.

## THE EEYOU

The ancient words are not easily translated into the modern Cree language. But they are understood in a spiritual way that unites the people with their past.

Songs are simple in form and words, but complex in emotional meanings. There is the "river rapids song," the "bear song," the "running song," the "hunting caribou song," and many, many more about the daily activities of the people.

Some songs express a hunter's feelings and give him inspiration and power. It is thought that this power helps him communicate with the animals. The Eeyou believe that the animals hear the song and feel a love and respect for the hunter. During the hunt, they believe, the animals let the hunter kill them.

This is a song the Eeyou used to sing when they started to hunt caribou in the fall:

> When I hunt caribou,
> I feel as if they are standing still
> even if they are running away from me,
> I feel as if they are standing still.
> How easy it is when I go to kill caribou.

## KEEPING THE LANGUAGE

Today the Eeyou have a written language. Stories and other information are being recorded in books. Instead of an alphabet, the Cree language is written in symbols that stand for syllables, sounds that make up parts of words. (See the syllabics chart on page 72.)

The Cree language is kept alive because the children learn it as babies and continue to speak only Cree in the early grades at school. Later in elementary school the children learn English and French. The Eeyou believe their children should speak non-native languages. They understand that they are part of a larger world. This knowledge will give the new generations the tools needed to defend their land and way of life.

## THE NEW GENERATION

Young Eeyou inherit a rich past and a challenge to keep the old ways during times of change. Today the newest generation of Eeyou are born in modern hospitals. But newborns are cared for using many traditional items.

A newborn is laced into a *wasbisooyan*, a special holder that can be carried around. During the day a baby naps in a *mamapsuhn*, or hammock. A mother lets her teething baby chew on goose and duck bones or pieces of smooth animal hide. Crushed fish is usually a baby's first food.

Traditionally, women collected **sphagnum moss** to use as diapers. This moss holds large amounts of water, keeping the skin dry and preventing rashes. When traveling in the bush, moss diapers are still used because the moss is the driest and warmest material available.

*While most Eeyou today are born in modern hospitals, babies still rest in the traditional* mamapsuhn, *a small hammock.*

## WALKING-OUT

When a baby can walk, he or she is ready for the Walking-out Ceremony. This ancient ceremony celebrates a child's introduction into Cree society.

The Walking-out Ceremony starts at daybreak. During the spring and summer families gather at a tent prepared especially for the ceremony. Fresh spruce boughs cover the ground both inside the tent and outside in a path around the woodpile.

The children are dressed in traditional clothing made of caribou and moose hide. Each boy carries a small wooden gun or bow and arrow. The girls carry toy snow shovels, axes, and small cooking sticks. These toys represent the real tools used by men and women. Every child also carries a small sack filled with traditional foods as well as sugar, tea, and tobacco.

The children line up at the door of the tent and walk out (with the help of their mothers). They follow the path of spruce boughs around the woodpile. In front of the woodpile the boys pretend to shoot their guns into the air, and the girls pretend to chop wood with their axes.

Inside the tent the elders are the first to welcome the children into the Cree society by kissing each child and taking his or her sack. An old man and woman open the sacks and pass the tobacco around for the men to smoke in their pipes. The women make a big fire and bring in the food for the *makussaan,* or feast.

## THE UNBROKEN CIRCLE

The Walking-out Ceremony is the first and one of the most important ceremonies in a person's life. It welcomes children into Cree society, and it also celebrates the work–hunting, cooking, caring for the fire, and chopping wood–that children will learn at a young age and do for the rest of their lives.

In the Cree culture a person's life cannot be broken into separate periods of childhood, adulthood, and old age. Instead, children learn and practice the same skills they will use as adults and elders. When a person is very old, he or she doesn't "retire" and move away from the family. Elders still take part in daily work, and their knowledge and experience are respected by all.

The Eeyou think of life as a circle. For example, a boy learns how to hunt by watching his father and other men. As he grows,

*Dressed in caribou skins, this little girl is ready for the Walking-out Ceremony. She carries a toy ax in her hand and small logs on her back, symbols of the work she will do as a woman.*

he also learns from his own experience. By the time he is a man, he is a good hunter, but he doesn't reach his peak until he is in his 40s or 50s. Then he slowly becomes less successful at hunting. But by this time his own sons are successful hunters.

## THE HUNTERS

Men do most of the hunting and trapping. This work requires them to travel into the bush for weeks at a time. Preparation and maintenance of tools, sleds, and showshoes are essential for successful hunting.

The Eeyou believe that a good hunter, or *naabaaw*, has many important qualities. For example, a *naabaaw* never talks about how he killed an animal, never boasts or brags, and never makes fun of a less successful hunter. A good hunter shares his catch generously, is modest, and manages to catch something even when animals or birds are scarce.

For the Eeyou, hunting is not a sport but a demanding and rewarding job. And the first important accomplishments made by young hunters are always celebrated. The Eeyou enjoy feasts when a boy receives his first gun, when he kills his first animal, and when he kills his first caribou.

## WOMEN'S WORK

Young girls also learn to hunt and trap, but the animals they kill are small. When a girl kills her first animal, the special day is celebrated. A part of the animal–a beak or jawbone–is decorated and passed around the teepee for all to admire. Then the people dip the animal part into a traditional food made from dried meat and crushed berries, and everyone eats from it.

Although it is important for women to know how to hunt, hunting is not their main activity. The women do most of the work at the winter camp. One of a woman's most important tasks is chopping wood. The Eeyou believe that if a woman is chopping

*A hunter makes tools he will use in the bush.*

wood, her husband will see many animals in the bush.

Twice a week the women cut fresh spruce boughs for the lodge floor. They cook, fetch water–or snow and ice to melt–sew, and thread snowshoes. And, as in most cultures, they care for the children.

When a hunter returns to the camp, his wife and children wait quietly inside the tent. This shows respect for the hunter.

*Stretching a beaver skin on a wooden frame, one of the many jobs Eeyou women do*

The first thing the woman does is take the hunting bag and look inside. Then she serves the man tea, even if he has brought back nothing.

Although there are separate tasks done by men and women, all work is respected as important. Some chores are shared by men and women alike. Both sexes carry game and set up the tents and lodges when arriving at a new camp.

Paddling canoes and portaging, or carrying the boats and supplies over land between rivers and lakes, are physically demanding tasks done by both women and men.

## THE BEAR'S PAW

Traditionally, all travel in the bush was extremely demanding.

*Making a fish net*

The Eeyou either paddled their own handmade canoes or walked on snowshoes between camps. Today motorized equipment has made bush travel much easier. However, people must still be skilled at using traditional methods of travel. Snowshoes and canoes can go many places that motorized vehicles can't—and they are much quieter.

A very old ceremony celebrates a child's ability to walk on snowshoes between winter camps. A young child walks on his

50

*Cleaning fish*

or her first pair of snowshoes and pulls a sled of food to a new camp. At the camp the child is kissed and everyone enjoys a feast.

The snowshoes used in this ceremony are made from birch or tamarack trees, and are constructed in the shape of a bear's paw. The Eeyou believe that the power of the bear will protect the child from danger.

Using bear-paw snowshoes is just one way the Eeyou symbolically connect themselves with animals. Almost every-thing they do involves a respect for the animals and land that provide them with food. Respect, in fact, is the essence of the Cree culture.

# CHAPTER FOUR

# RESPECT FOR ALL

ᒥᓯᐌᔨᐦᑐ

Surviving in the harsh subarctic environment requires cooperation among people. Each person has an important role to perform, which helps the entire group prosper. Respect for one another is a way of recognizing the important contributions made by each person.

Elders are the most respected people, and old women are the most highly regarded of all. Special places are reserved for old men and women inside the camp. An old woman's place is nearest the door, or *ishkawtem*. This place is kept clean and comfortable. When the woman goes out, she will always bring wood back into the camp. This is important because the wood is a symbol of the animals she attracts to the hunters. Even though the woman is old, she still takes part in the hunting by bringing in wood.

An old man's place is at the back of the camp, opposite the exit. This place is called *waaskwaataam*. Animals are skinned and important rituals take place here, such as cracking the knuckles of black bears. When a black bear is brought to camp, it is placed next to the old man. This shows respect to the man and to the bear.

*A Cree elder. Elders never "retire" from the community but remain important and respected members of society.*

# THE EEYOU

The Eeyou believe that animals as well as people show respect. In the following tale a whale pays tribute to a hunter:

This old man was a respected hunter. He even went to Whapmagoostui (Great Whale River) to hunt beluga whales and he was very good at it. . . . One time he was on the First Rapids of the La Grande River, camping with his family. His grandchildren were playing outside. They saw a beluga whale come up to the rapids. Just then, the old man passed away. There are many true stories of certain animals coming to pay tribute to a great hunter just before his death.

## RESPECT FOR THE ANIMALS

When an animal is killed, its flesh nourishes the people. Animals are so important to the Eeyou that many customs and beliefs have come about to help ensure the success of the hunters.

One custom is for hunters to show humility in front of an animal. A humble–not boastful or proud–attitude will, the Eeyou believe, pacify the animal's spirit. Then the animal will allow the hunter to kill it.

Also, when a hunter approaches an animal, he does so calmly and quietly. For example, if he has found a black bear's den, he announces his arrival to the bear: "I am here," he says, and then he kills the bear quickly.

The first thing a hunter does after killing a bear is check how much fat there is under the skin on its chest. Animals with high fat content are considered healthy. If an animal appears to have been sick, the body is burned.

A single hunter often carries a bear to camp on his back, piggyback style. The bear's paws hang over the man's shoulders and are tied to its legs, which are held under the hunter's arms. Two men sometimes carry a bear on a pole with the bear's limbs tied together.

At the camp, rituals are held and offerings are made to the bear. Bears require special respect because they are important, powerful animals. When a bear is killed, the hunters gather in a circle at the camp and smoke tobacco. They put some tobacco leaves in the bear's mouth. A piece of bear meat and some tobacco leaves are thrown into the fire as an offering. By making an offering, a hunter is asking the bear to give more game in the future. An offering is also a way of thanking the creator for the bear.

In another ritual, the hunters try to crack the bear's knuckles. If the knuckles crack, the Eeyou believe the bear had been hiding game from the hunter in the past. Cracking the knuckles breaks the spell, and the hunter will have more luck in the future.

Every animal is killed, carried, and cut in different ways. When a bear is skinned, the men make the first cuts. Then the women skin the bear and the men cut off the limbs. The man who killed the bear decides how to give the meat away. Usually a hunter asks an elder to give the meat to the rest of the people. This shows respect to the bear.

Every person, including babies, gets an equal share of bear meat. The next day everyone shares the meat that was saved for the babies. Bear meat can be eaten only at the camp. The Eeyou believe it would be disrespectful to eat the meat while away checking traps or hunting.

After the Eeyou have eaten the bear meat, they perform a final ritual, similar to a burial. The skull and other bones are hung in trees or placed on wooden platforms several feet above the ground. The Eeyou believe that the spirit of the bear is now free to return to the bush and be born again in another bear.

## WASTE NOT

The most important rule concerning animals is that nothing be wasted. When an animal is killed, all of it must be eaten or used to make clothing and other items. Even when boys are learning to hunt, they are not allowed to kill animals just for fun or practice. The animal is cooked and eaten, no matter how small.

In traditional Cree cooking, all parts of an animal are used. Blood, for example, is made into puddings or used in stews. However, there are exceptions–the Eeyou do not eat polar bear liver because it is poisonous.

## SHARING THE WEALTH

The Eeyou believe that the wealth of the land should be shared among all the people. This ensures the survival of the community.

*Rabbit skins hanging from a tree. The Eeyou never kill animals just for fun, and they make sure to use all parts of an animal, no matter how small it is.*

# THE EEYOU

If one hunter does not bring in animals for several days, his family will be fed by other hunters who have had more luck. This sharing bonds people together.

The Eeyou follow many rituals when sharing food. Specific parts of certain animals may only be eaten by certain groups of people. For example, only men are allowed to eat the head of the bear and only women may eat the backbone. Old men are allowed to eat the bones with the attached meat. Children are not allowed to eat the limbs. The Eeyou believe that if a child eats from a bear's limb, she or he will get old too quickly. Although these rules may be considered superstitious, nearly every culture has rituals about food.

Knowledge is also shared among the people. For example, knowledge of medicines and medical treatments is not restricted to a few individuals, although the Eeyou do have **shamans**. These "medicine men" are consulted in special cases.

The Eeyou often give gifts of medicines to one another. They are made from animal fats and plants such as birch bark, balsam needles, and cattail roots.

In the past the Eeyou had few health problems. Their life in the bush provided them with pure water, fresh food, and plenty of exercise. During the past 30 years, the changes brought by living more in the village and less in the bush have caused health problems for some people. These diseases, such as heart disease and diabetes, were unknown in traditional Cree society.

*Sunset in northern Quebec: The Eeyou have respect for the land and all living things.*

Today the Eeyou require modern medicines, such as anti-biotics, to treat new diseases introduced by outsiders. However, they still use many traditional remedies for common injuries or illnesses.

## RESPECT FOR THE EARTH

Probably more important than the continued use of traditional medicines are the ideas the Eeyou have kept about health and life. The Eeyou believe that just as the body must be cared for so that it remains healthy and in balance, so must the earth. This respect for nature has preserved their way of life and their lands for thousands of years.

# CHAPTER FIVE

# THE GLOBAL VILLAGE

△ᐢ·Ċ °  Today I stand on the land I used to hunt on, but now there's a town that Hydro has built. It is here that my child was born, and it is here where my ancestors lie. It is on this land that my dad hunted. He left no sign of his presence and I left no sign of my presence.

For years I have depended upon the land as a means of survival. I am told that now the fish nearby are contaminated with mercury. I am told not to eat the fish. How can I just stop eating it when for years I have lived off it? Who would eat something that they were told has poison in it? I am pretty sure nobody would! How is this justifiable?

–Words from a Cree elder

The new town that the Cree elder is speaking about is called Chisasibi. It was built by Hydro-Quebec on the mainland to replace the old village of Fort George, located on an island in the mouth of the La Grande River. Upstream from Fort George is a huge hydroelectric power station that has changed the way the river flows around the island and into the bay.

Fort George was originally a summer gathering place. Later

*This massive spillway is part of the La Grande Complex and carries water out of the reservoir during spring floods and fall rains. Each of the 13 steps in the spillway is as wide as 1½ football fields and as high as two telephone poles.*

it became a permanent village. Today some Eeyou have refused to move away from Fort George to settle in Chisasibi.

Other places have been totally destroyed by dams and **reservoirs**. Along the first rapids of the La Grande are rocks from which people fished for generations. Today a power station stands on them. No longer a place for gathering, the ancient rocks represent part of the Cree culture lost forever.

There are seven power stations in the La Grande project, and the government plans to build more. Some 4,425 square miles of hunting territory and sacred burial grounds are under water, an area equal to the state of Connecticut. And at least six times as much land has been affected by the flooding.

THE EEYOU

## ENERGY FOR THE WORLD

One of the most important needs of the industrialized world is energy. Energy is required to run factories and to light and heat buildings. And the homeland of the Eeyou is rich in energy.

The kinetic energy, or the energy of motion, found in the rushing waters of the huge rivers flowing into James Bay can be changed into electricity. This electricity is transmitted by high-voltage wires to cities hundreds of miles away.

Many people think of electricity generated by waterpower as "clean" energy because fossil fuels are not burned. But for the Eeyou, hydroelectric power has created problems that threaten their way of life.

## "FISH DISEASE"

Some problems are very obvious, such as contaminated fish and water birds. When land is flooded, a poisonous chemical called methylmercury seeps out of drowned trees and plants. The chemical reaction that creates the methylmercury is part of the natural process of underwater decay.

In the James Bay area millions of acres of trees were covered by water. As fish and water birds in the artificial lakes feed off the poisonous, rotting plants, mercury becomes concentrated in their flesh. When the Eeyou eat these animals, they get sick.

Hydro-Quebec officials say the problem will go away in 30 years, but no one really knows. What the Eeyou do know is that

*Someday these rushing waters along the Great Whale River may be dammed to produce electricity for people hundreds of miles away.*

an essential part of their diet and way of life has been lost.

## LOST LAND, LOST RIVERS

Other problems have been created by flooding the land, such as the destruction of wildlife habitat along rivers. Before the area was flooded, it provided important feeding and breeding grounds for caribou, beavers, migratory birds, and many other kinds of animals hunted and trapped by the Eeyou.

The way rivers normally flow has been changed, too. The Eastmain River has been diverted, or changed to flow in a different direction than it normally would. Now it flows into the La Grande River instead of into James Bay. As a result, the Eastmain has 90 percent less water in it, and the La Grande carries twice as much water as it did before the project.

During the winter, water is released from dams to produce more electricity for heating buildings in Montreal and the northeastern United States. Instead of normal floods from melting snows in spring, the rivers flood in the winter. In 1984, 10,000 caribou drowned as they were trying to cross the river during an artificially produced flood. Winter flooding also changes water temperatures and salt levels along the James Bay coast. The result is an **ecosystem** out of balance.

## THE LONGEST ROAD

Some changes and problems are not caused directly by the

dams and flooding, but by the roads that have been built to bring in equipment, supplies, and workers. Today anyone can travel into the once-isolated land of the Eeyou.

A new road, Route 109, connects the La Grande River to Montreal. Trophy hunters, hundreds of miles from their homes, travel north in search of bear, moose, and caribou. The Eeyou depend on these big-game animals for food, and now they must compete with sportsmen.

Loggers have also invaded the forests, **clear-cutting** trees, causing **erosion**, and polluting rivers and lakes with oil and gas. Mining companies are pressing north looking for copper, zinc, silver, uranium, iron, chrome, and gold.

The roads also bring rapid change and serious problems to the small villages. Drug and alcohol abuse, divorce, and suicide were once unknown in Cree society.

Not all Cree villages are connected by road to the outside world. Whapmagoostui, or Great Whale River, is the northern-most Cree village. The only way to get there is by plane, but that could change soon. Hydro-Quebec wants to build a road to Whapmagoostui and construct dams and power stations along the rapids of the Great Whale River.

## BROKEN PROMISES

When the Eeyou signed the James Bay and Northern Quebec Agreement, they believed there would be no more hydroelectric projects without their consent and approval. But the agreement has not been honored, and Hydro-Quebec plans to build James Bay II.

James Bay II would dam five rivers as part of the Great Whale River Project and would also dam the Nottaway, Broadback, and Rupert rivers as part of the NBR Project. If James Bay II is completed, all the major rivers in northern Quebec would be changed forever.

The Eeyou in Whapmagoostui fear the same problems the Eeyou in Chisasibi are facing now. Mercury poisoning, winter flooding, and destruction of the habitats of caribou and migratory birds would occur. Other animals unique to the northern region, such as freshwater seals and beluga whales, would be threatened. And the ancient and sacred burial grounds of the Eeyou would be flooded and destroyed forever.

## WORKING TOGETHER

The 500 Eeyou who live in Whapmagoostui share their village with 500 Inuit. The Inuit call the village Kuutjuaraapik. These two groups of indigenous people have united to oppose James Bay II. In April of 1990 the people made a historic voyage from Hudson Bay, down the Hudson River, and all the way to New York City. They paddled their boat, the *Odeyak*, into New York on Earth Day. And they brought with them a message for New Yorkers and other Americans.

*The village of Whapmagoostui along the Great Whale River and Hudson Bay. Future hydroelectric projects threaten to flood this region and disrupt its ecosystem.*

The Eeyou and Inuit made many people aware that Americans are contributing to the destruction of their ancient cultures by using electricity generated in James Bay. As a result, groups were formed in the United States to protest the hydroelectric projects. And in 1992 New York State decided not to buy any electricity from James Bay II. Many scientists believe that the huge hydroelectric projects could be avoided if energy **conservation** programs were developed instead.

## KEEPERS OF THE FIRE

Today there are more than 10,000 Eeyou. And most of the people are young–under 25 years old. Many of the new generation want to live traditional lives in the bush, but the land can support only a limited number of hunters. Therefore, not all Eeyou will be able to live in the bush as their ancestors did. However, the Eeyou believe that their culture can thrive into the 21st century if they are the people who decide the future of their ancient lands.

As they fight for control of their lands, the Eeyou also defend their traditional way of life. They guard their language, skills, customs, and rituals in the same careful way that fire was guarded long, long ago.

Fire was guarded because, if it went out, it could only be started again by striking two pieces of rock together, which took a long time. When traveling from one camp to another, someone had to carry a smoldering log, usually in a wooden bucket or dried bear stomach. This person, the fire keeper, had to blow on the log to keep the fire going. When the camp was set up again, the fire keeper put the log in the fire pit at the center of the teepee and started a new fire.

Today the culture of the Eeyou is like the ancient fire. And the Eeyou, each one of them, are the fire keepers. They are the elders who tell traditional stories and sing ancient songs. They are the young hunters, men and women, who live traditional lives in the bush. They are the chiefs who lead the people in their

*The future of the Eeyou depends on everyone.*

struggle for self-government and control of their native lands. They are the parents and teachers who help children make sense of two worlds–traditional and modern. But the most important fire keepers of all are the children, because they are the ones who will carry their ancient culture into and beyond the next century.

# IN THE BUSH CAMP

In the Bush Camp
there's no electricity, no houses, no TV
and no Nintendo.

In the Bush Camp,
I can go hunting and trapping
for beaver, otter and rabbit.

I can use the canoe for hunting and placing fishnets.
I look around the bush in the fall.

In the winter, I can ride the Ski-Doo in the bush
and look for grouse, ptarmigan, caribou, moose, beaver,
porcupine and all other kinds of animals.

I also can get wood and boughs or play for amusement.
I look at the beautiful scenery in the forest.

When I look for a grouse,
I look in the forest.
I look for it under the tree or
somewhere on the middle of the tree.

When I look for ptarmigan,
I look for it in the shrubs or
somewhere on the hills or on the sand.
When it's cold,
I look somewhere where it is warm.

When I look for a beaver,
I look into the streams or in the ponds.
I also look for beaver lodges and beaver dams.

When I look for caribou or moose,
I look on the mountains or
somewhere where there's moss.

When I look for a bear,
I look up or down the hills
where there are lots of berries,
in the mountain or in the cave.

When I look for boughs,
I get them from spruce trees
and I get wood from dead or dry trees in the forest.

This is what I do at Bush Camp.


**–Lindy Rupert, Badabin Eeyou School, Whapmagoostui**

# EEYOU SYLLABICS CHART

| | e | we | i | ii | u | uu | a | aa | waa | Final | Final |
|---|---|---|---|---|---|---|---|---|---|---|---|
| | e | | i | ii | u | uu | a | aa | | u | h |
| | we | | wi | wii | wu | wuu | wa | waa | | | |
| p | pe | pwe | pi | pii | pu | puu | pa | paa | pwaa | p | |
| t | te | twe | ti | tii | tu | tuu | ta | taa | twaa | t | |
| k | ke | kwe | ki | kii | ku | kuu | ka | kaa | kwaa | k | kw |
| ch | che | chwe | chi | chii | chu | chuu | cha | chaa | chwaa | ch | |
| l | le | | li | lii | lu | luu | la | laa | lwaa | l | |
| m | me | mwe | mi | mii | mu | muu | ma | maa | mwaa | m | mw |
| n | ne | nwe | ni | nii | nu | nuu | na | naa | nwaa | n | |
| r | re | | ri | rii | ru | ruu | ra | raa | rwaa | r | |
| s | se | swe | si | sii | su | suu | sa | saa | swaa | s | |
| sh | she | shwe | shi | shii | shu | shuu | sha | shaa | shwaa | sh | |
| y | ye | ywe | yi | yii | yu | yuu | ya | yaa | ywaa | y | |
| v | ve | | vi | vii | vu | vuu | va | vaa | vwaa | v | |
| th | the | | thi | thii | thu | thuu | tha | thaa | thwaa | th | |

Finals

# ACTIVITIES

**1.** <u>Learn about the Cree language.</u> At the beginning of each chapter there are words written in the Cree language. Find out what the Cree words mean by matching them with the Cree dictionary below. Try to pronounce the words using the Eeyou syllabics chart on page 72. Try to write the words using the symbols.

### CREE DICTIONARY

ᓂᑎᐸᐃᑖᓐ *nitibaaihtaan*–to take care of the land and animals, as a steward or custodian

ᒥᒋᓲ     *michisuu*–eagle

ᓈᐹᐤ     *naabaaw*–a man; a proper hunter

ᒋᔖᔮᒄ    *chishaayaakw*–black bear

ᐃᔅᑖᐤ    *istwaau*–conservation; literally, "he is saving it for later use"

**2.** <u>Learn about the indigenous people who lived or live in your area.</u> Start your research at the library or local museum. Find out the names of the Indian tribes that lived in your state and county. Contact local organizations that have information about the group of people you are studying. If native people still live in your area, contact their representatives and ask them if they have any information they can send you about their culture. Learn more by visiting members of their community and listening to them speak about their traditions.

**3.** <u>Send letters to the Eeyou.</u> Tell them why you support them and how learning about their culture has influenced the way you think. Ask them what they would like non-native people to do to support them in their effort to save their lands and way of life.

    If you would like to write to Cree students, send letters to:

      Susan Runnels
      Education Services
      Chisasibi, Quebec J0M 1E0
      Canada

For more information or to send your support, write:

Cree School Board
282 Main Street
P.O. Box 1210
Mistissini, Quebec G0W 1C0
Canada

Grand Council of the
Crees of Quebec
24 Bayswater Avenue
Ottawa, Ontario K1Y 2E4
Canada

James Bay Cultural Education Centre
Box 390
Chisasibi, Quebec J0M 1E0
Canada

Cree Trappers Association
1440 de la Quebecoise
Val d'Or, Quebec J9P 5H4
Canada

**4.** Learn more about organizations working to help the Eeyou or other indigenous people save their culture and lands. Write to one or more of the following organizations and ask them to send you information about what they are doing to protect James Bay from further development.

## ORGANIZATIONS

Cultural Survival (Canada)
Suite 420
1 Nicholas Street
Ottawa, Ontario, K1N 7B7
Canada

Cultural Survival (USA)
215 First Street
Cambridge, MA 02142

National Audubon Society
700 Broadway
New York, NY 10003

PROTECT
P.O. Box 203
Goshen, NY 10924

Sierra Club
730 Polk Street
San Francisco, CA 94109

Survival International
310 Edgeware Road
London W2 1DY
United Kingdom

# FOR FURTHER READING

*Earthmaker's Tales: North American Indian Stories about Earth Happenings*, by Gretchen Will Mayo. New York: Walker and Company, 1989.

*James Bay Memoirs: A Cree Woman's Ode to Her Homeland*, by Margaret Cromarty. Ontario, Canada: Waapoone Publishing and Promotion, 1992.

*Keepers of the Animals*, by Michael Caduto and Joseph Bruchac. Golden, Colo.: Fulcrum, Inc., 1991.

*Keepers of the Earth*, by Michael Caduto and Joseph Bruchac. Golden, Colo: Fulcrum, Inc., 1988.

*Millenium: Tribal Wisdom and the Modern World*, by David Maybury-Lewis. New York: Viking, 1992.

*Pueblo Storyteller*, by Diane Hoyt-Goldsmith, New York: Holiday House, 1991.

*The Rough-Face Girl*, by Rafe Martin. New York: Putnam, 1992.

*The Sacred Path: Spells, Prayers and Power Songs of the American Indians*, John Bierhorst ed. New York: William Morrow and Company, 1983.

*Teaching Kids to Love the Earth*, by Marina Lachecki Herman, Joseph F. Passineau, Ann L. Schimpf, and Paul Treuer. Duluth, Minn.: Pfeifer-Hamilton, 1991.

*That's What She Said: Contemporary Poetry and Fiction by Native American Women*, Rayna Green ed. Bloomington, Ind.: Indiana University Press, 1988.

# GLOSSARY

**bog**–a wetland formed by the glaciers in which water does not flow in or out; characterized by sphagnum moss and other specialized plants.

**bush**–the wild and uncleared forests where the Eeyou hunt, trap, and fish.

**clear-cutting**–logging or harvesting all the trees in a forest so that nothing is left but stumps.

**conservation**–the practice of saving something for the future.

**culture**–the complete way of living, including ideas, customs, skills, and arts, of a people.

**ecosystem**–all the living and nonliving things in a certain area.

**elder**–an older person with authority and dignity in a community.

**erosion**–a wearing, washing, or eating away. Trees and grass help prevent the erosion of soil by protecting it from the wind and rain.

**game**–wild birds or animals hunted for food or sport.

**global village**–the entire modern world in which diverse people communicate, share experiences, and depend on one another for resources.

**hibernating**–spending the winter in a resting or sleeping state.

**hunter-gatherers**–people who survive by hunting animals and gathering plants for food.

**indigenous**–native to a region; indigenous people are the descendants of the first people to settle a region; they are also called native, original, aboriginal, or first peoples.

**migratory**–birds, animals, or people that wander over a large area in search of food or places to give birth.

**missionaries**–people who are sent by their churches to a foreign country to preach, teach, and convert indigenous people to their religious faith.

**reservoirs**–artificial lakes formed when a river is dammed.

**rituals**–ceremonies, rites, or religious observances practiced by a culture, usually at specific times or intervals.

**shaman**–a priest who cures diseases by using supernatural powers in order to banish evil spirits from the body; also called a "medicine man."

**sphagnum moss**–spongy and highly absorbent plants that grow in bogs.

**Stone Age**–the earliest period in human culture; during the Stone Age people developed stone tools and weapons.

**subarctic**–the region surrounding the Arctic Circle.

**traditional**–according to tradition; doing things in the same ways as one's ancestors.

**traditions**–stories, beliefs, and customs that have been handed down from generation to generation.

**tribe**–a group of people who have the same ancestors, social customs, and other characteristics.

**tundra**–the treeless land found in arctic regions.

**voyageurs**–people who transported men and supplies by boat to the trading posts for the fur companies.

# SELECTED BIBLIOGRAPHY

## BOOKS

*Cree Trappers Speak.* Cree Trappers Association's Committee of Chisasibi (Joab Bearskin, George Lameboy, Robbie Matthew, Sr., Joseph Pepabano, Abraham Pisinaquan, William Ratt, and Daniel Rupert). James Bay Cree Cultural Education Centre: Chisasibi, Quebec. 1989.

Marshall, Susan and Lizzie Diamond, with Sarah Blackned. *Healing Ourselves, Helping Ourselves: The Medicinal Use of Plants and Animals by the People of Waskaganish.* Cree Regional Authority: Val d'Or, Quebec. 1989.

Newman, Peter C. *Empire of the Bay.* Penguin Books: Toronto. 1989.

Newton, Joanne Willis. *Aatiyuuhkaan: Legends of the Eastern James Bay Cree.* Text adaptation by Joanne Willis Newton. James Bay Cree Cultural Education Centre: Chisasibi, Quebec. 1989.

_____.*Once Upon This Land: The Legend of Aayaasaau.* Text adaptation by Joanne Willis Newton (English) and Luci Bobbish-Salt (Cree). James Bay Cree Cultural Education Centre, Chisasibi: Quebec, Canada. 1990.

Pachano, Jane. *Changing Times: Baby William; Changing Times: Bobby and Mary at Home; Changing Times: Clothing.* James Bay Cree Cultural Education Centre: Chisasibi, Quebec.1985.

_____. *Cree Customs: Walking Out Ceremony.* James Bay Cree Cultural Education Centre: Chisasibi, Quebec. 1984.

_____. *Waupsh.* James Bay Cree Cultural Education Centre: Chisasibi, Quebec. 1984.

Richardson, Boyce. *Strangers Devour the Land.* Chelsea Green Publishing: Post Mills, Vermont. 1991.

Salisbury, Richard F. *A Homeland for the Cree.* McGill-Queens's University Press: Montreal. 1986.

# INDEX

# ABOUT THE AUTHOR

Alexandra Siy's interest in the natural world began during the first celebration of Earth Day, when she was ten years old. She studied biology in college and went on to do research in a biotechnology laboratory. Later she earned a master's degree in science education and taught high school biology and physiology.

Ms. Siy, who lives in Albany, New York, now divides her time between writing and raising her two young children. **Global Villages** continues the theme of the interconnectedness of people and the environment, which she began in the **Circle of Life**, her first group of books for Dillon Press.